BUDGET PLANNER

This book belongs to :

_____

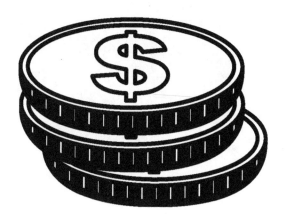

BUDGET *Planner*

MONTH:

STARTING BALANCE: _____

INCOME

DESCRIPTION	BUDGET	ACTUAL
TOTAL:		

SAVINGS

DESCRIPTION	BUDGET
TOTAL:	

EXPENSES

DESCRIPTION	BUDGET	ACTUAL	DIFFERENCE
TOTAL:			

BUDGET *Planner*

MONTH:

STARTING BALANCE: _____

INCOME

DESCRIPTION	BUDGET	ACTUAL
TOTAL:		

SAVINGS

DESCRIPTION	BUDGET
TOTAL:	

EXPENSES

DESCRIPTION	BUDGET	ACTUAL	DIFFERENCE
TOTAL:			

BUDGET *Planner*

MONTH:

STARTING BALANCE: _____

INCOME

DESCRIPTION	BUDGET	ACTUAL
TOTAL:		

SAVINGS

DESCRIPTION	BUDGET
TOTAL:	

EXPENSES

DESCRIPTION	BUDGET	ACTUAL	DIFFERENCE
TOTAL:			

BUDGET *Planner*

MONTH:

STARTING BALANCE: _____

INCOME				SAVINGS	
DESCRIPTION	BUDGET	ACTUAL		DESCRIPTION	BUDGET
TOTAL:				TOTAL:	

EXPENSES			
DESCRIPTION	BUDGET	ACTUAL	DIFFERENCE
TOTAL:			

BUDGET *Planner*

MONTH: _____

STARTING BALANCE: _____

INCOME			SAVINGS	
DESCRIPTION	BUDGET	ACTUAL	DESCRIPTION	BUDGET
TOTAL:			TOTAL:	

EXPENSES			
DESCRIPTION	BUDGET	ACTUAL	DIFFERENCE
TOTAL:			

BUDGET *Planner*

MONTH: _____

STARTING BALANCE: _____

INCOME

DESCRIPTION	BUDGET	ACTUAL
TOTAL:		

SAVINGS

DESCRIPTION	BUDGET
TOTAL:	

EXPENSES

DESCRIPTION	BUDGET	ACTUAL	DIFFERENCE
TOTAL:			

BUDGET *Planner*

MONTH:

STARTING BALANCE: _____

INCOME

DESCRIPTION	BUDGET	ACTUAL
TOTAL:		

SAVINGS

DESCRIPTION	BUDGET
TOTAL:	

EXPENSES

DESCRIPTION	BUDGET	ACTUAL	DIFFERENCE
TOTAL:			

BUDGET *Planner*

MONTH:

STARTING BALANCE: _____

INCOME

DESCRIPTION	BUDGET	ACTUAL
TOTAL:		

SAVINGS

DESCRIPTION	BUDGET
TOTAL:	

EXPENSES

DESCRIPTION	BUDGET	ACTUAL	DIFFERENCE
TOTAL:			

BUDGET *Planner*

MONTH:

STARTING BALANCE: _____

INCOME

DESCRIPTION	BUDGET	ACTUAL
TOTAL:		

SAVINGS

DESCRIPTION	BUDGET
TOTAL:	

EXPENSES

DESCRIPTION	BUDGET	ACTUAL	DIFFERENCE
TOTAL:			

BUDGET *Planner*

MONTH:

STARTING BALANCE: _____

INCOME		
DESCRIPTION	BUDGET	ACTUAL
TOTAL:		

SAVINGS	
DESCRIPTION	BUDGET
TOTAL:	

EXPENSES			
DESCRIPTION	BUDGET	ACTUAL	DIFFERENCE
TOTAL:			

BUDGET *Planner*

MONTH:

STARTING BALANCE: _____

INCOME

DESCRIPTION	BUDGET	ACTUAL
TOTAL:		

SAVINGS

DESCRIPTION	BUDGET
TOTAL:	

EXPENSES

DESCRIPTION	BUDGET	ACTUAL	DIFFERENCE
TOTAL:			

BUDGET *Planner*

MONTH:

STARTING BALANCE: _____

INCOME

DESCRIPTION	BUDGET	ACTUAL
TOTAL:		

SAVINGS

DESCRIPTION	BUDGET
TOTAL:	

EXPENSES

DESCRIPTION	BUDGET	ACTUAL	DIFFERENCE
TOTAL:			

BUDGET *Planner*

MONTH:

STARTING BALANCE: _____

INCOME

DESCRIPTION	BUDGET	ACTUAL
TOTAL:		

SAVINGS

DESCRIPTION	BUDGET
TOTAL:	

EXPENSES

DESCRIPTION	BUDGET	ACTUAL	DIFFERENCE
TOTAL:			

BUDGET *Planner*

STARTING BALANCE: _____

INCOME

DESCRIPTION	BUDGET	ACTUAL
TOTAL:		

SAVINGS

DESCRIPTION	BUDGET
TOTAL:	

EXPENSES

DESCRIPTION	BUDGET	ACTUAL	DIFFERENCE
TOTAL:			

BUDGET *Planner*

MONTH:

STARTING BALANCE: _____

INCOME

DESCRIPTION	BUDGET	ACTUAL
TOTAL:		

SAVINGS

DESCRIPTION	BUDGET
TOTAL:	

EXPENSES

DESCRIPTION	BUDGET	ACTUAL	DIFFERENCE
TOTAL:			

BUDGET *Planner*

MONTH:

STARTING BALANCE: _____

INCOME

DESCRIPTION	BUDGET	ACTUAL
TOTAL:		

SAVINGS

DESCRIPTION	BUDGET
TOTAL:	

EXPENSES

DESCRIPTION	BUDGET	ACTUAL	DIFFERENCE
TOTAL:			

BUDGET *Planner*

MONTH:

STARTING BALANCE: _____

INCOME		
DESCRIPTION	BUDGET	ACTUAL
TOTAL:		

SAVINGS	
DESCRIPTION	BUDGET
TOTAL:	

EXPENSES			
DESCRIPTION	BUDGET	ACTUAL	DIFFERENCE
TOTAL:			

BUDGET *Planner*

MONTH:

STARTING BALANCE: _____

INCOME			SAVINGS	
DESCRIPTION	BUDGET	ACTUAL	DESCRIPTION	BUDGET
TOTAL:			TOTAL:	

EXPENSES			
DESCRIPTION	BUDGET	ACTUAL	DIFFERENCE
TOTAL:			

BUDGET *Planner*

STARTING BALANCE: _____

INCOME

DESCRIPTION	BUDGET	ACTUAL
TOTAL:		

SAVINGS

DESCRIPTION	BUDGET
TOTAL:	

EXPENSES

DESCRIPTION	BUDGET	ACTUAL	DIFFERENCE
TOTAL:			

BUDGET *Planner*

MONTH:

STARTING BALANCE: _____

INCOME		
DESCRIPTION	BUDGET	ACTUAL
TOTAL:		

SAVINGS	
DESCRIPTION	BUDGET
TOTAL:	

EXPENSES			
DESCRIPTION	BUDGET	ACTUAL	DIFFERENCE
TOTAL:			

BUDGET *Planner*

MONTH:

STARTING BALANCE:

INCOME

DESCRIPTION	BUDGET	ACTUAL
TOTAL:		

SAVINGS

DESCRIPTION	BUDGET
TOTAL:	

EXPENSES

DESCRIPTION	BUDGET	ACTUAL	DIFFERENCE
TOTAL:			

BUDGET *Planner*

MONTH:

STARTING BALANCE: _____

INCOME

DESCRIPTION	BUDGET	ACTUAL
TOTAL:		

SAVINGS

DESCRIPTION	BUDGET
TOTAL:	

EXPENSES

DESCRIPTION	BUDGET	ACTUAL	DIFFERENCE
TOTAL:			

BUDGET *Planner*

MONTH:

STARTING BALANCE: _____

INCOME

DESCRIPTION	BUDGET	ACTUAL

TOTAL:

SAVINGS

DESCRIPTION	BUDGET

TOTAL:

EXPENSES

DESCRIPTION	BUDGET	ACTUAL	DIFFERENCE

TOTAL:

BUDGET *Planner*

MONTH:

STARTING BALANCE: _____

INCOME

DESCRIPTION	BUDGET	ACTUAL
TOTAL:		

SAVINGS

DESCRIPTION	BUDGET
TOTAL:	

EXPENSES

DESCRIPTION	BUDGET	ACTUAL	DIFFERENCE
TOTAL:			

BUDGET *Planner*

MONTH:

STARTING BALANCE: _____

INCOME				SAVINGS	
DESCRIPTION	BUDGET	ACTUAL		DESCRIPTION	BUDGET
TOTAL:				TOTAL:	

EXPENSES			
DESCRIPTION	BUDGET	ACTUAL	DIFFERENCE
TOTAL:			

BUDGET *Planner*

MONTH:

STARTING BALANCE: _____

INCOME

DESCRIPTION	BUDGET	ACTUAL
TOTAL:		

SAVINGS

DESCRIPTION	BUDGET
TOTAL:	

EXPENSES

DESCRIPTION	BUDGET	ACTUAL	DIFFERENCE
TOTAL:			

BUDGET *Planner*

MONTH:

STARTING BALANCE: _____

INCOME

DESCRIPTION	BUDGET	ACTUAL
TOTAL:		

SAVINGS

DESCRIPTION	BUDGET
TOTAL:	

EXPENSES

DESCRIPTION	BUDGET	ACTUAL	DIFFERENCE
TOTAL:			

BUDGET *Planner*

MONTH:

STARTING BALANCE: _____

INCOME

DESCRIPTION	BUDGET	ACTUAL
TOTAL:		

SAVINGS

DESCRIPTION	BUDGET
TOTAL:	

EXPENSES

DESCRIPTION	BUDGET	ACTUAL	DIFFERENCE
TOTAL:			

BUDGET *Planner*

MONTH:

STARTING BALANCE: _____

INCOME				SAVINGS	
DESCRIPTION	BUDGET	ACTUAL		DESCRIPTION	BUDGET
TOTAL:				TOTAL:	

EXPENSES			
DESCRIPTION	BUDGET	ACTUAL	DIFFERENCE
TOTAL:			

BUDGET *Planner*

MONTH:

STARTING BALANCE: _____

INCOME

DESCRIPTION	BUDGET	ACTUAL
TOTAL:		

SAVINGS

DESCRIPTION	BUDGET
TOTAL:	

EXPENSES

DESCRIPTION	BUDGET	ACTUAL	DIFFERENCE
TOTAL:			

BUDGET *Planner*

MONTH:

STARTING BALANCE: _____

INCOME

DESCRIPTION	BUDGET	ACTUAL
TOTAL:		

SAVINGS

DESCRIPTION	BUDGET
TOTAL:	

EXPENSES

DESCRIPTION	BUDGET	ACTUAL	DIFFERENCE
TOTAL:			

BUDGET *Planner*

MONTH:

STARTING BALANCE: _____

INCOME

DESCRIPTION	BUDGET	ACTUAL
TOTAL:		

SAVINGS

DESCRIPTION	BUDGET
TOTAL:	

EXPENSES

DESCRIPTION	BUDGET	ACTUAL	DIFFERENCE
TOTAL:			

BUDGET *Planner*

MONTH:

STARTING BALANCE: _____

INCOME

DESCRIPTION	BUDGET	ACTUAL
TOTAL:		

SAVINGS

DESCRIPTION	BUDGET
TOTAL:	

EXPENSES

DESCRIPTION	BUDGET	ACTUAL	DIFFERENCE
TOTAL:			

BUDGET *Planner*

MONTH: _____

STARTING BALANCE: _____

INCOME			SAVINGS	
DESCRIPTION	BUDGET	ACTUAL	DESCRIPTION	BUDGET
TOTAL:			TOTAL:	

EXPENSES			
DESCRIPTION	BUDGET	ACTUAL	DIFFERENCE
TOTAL:			

BUDGET *Planner*

MONTH:

STARTING BALANCE: _____

INCOME

DESCRIPTION	BUDGET	ACTUAL
TOTAL:		

SAVINGS

DESCRIPTION	BUDGET
TOTAL:	

EXPENSES

DESCRIPTION	BUDGET	ACTUAL	DIFFERENCE
TOTAL:			

BUDGET *Planner*

MONTH:

STARTING BALANCE: _____

INCOME

DESCRIPTION	BUDGET	ACTUAL
TOTAL:		

SAVINGS

DESCRIPTION	BUDGET
TOTAL:	

EXPENSES

DESCRIPTION	BUDGET	ACTUAL	DIFFERENCE
TOTAL:			

BUDGET *Planner*

MONTH:

STARTING BALANCE: _____

INCOME

DESCRIPTION	BUDGET	ACTUAL
TOTAL:		

SAVINGS

DESCRIPTION	BUDGET
TOTAL:	

EXPENSES

DESCRIPTION	BUDGET	ACTUAL	DIFFERENCE
TOTAL:			

BUDGET *Planner*

MONTH:

STARTING BALANCE: _____

INCOME

DESCRIPTION	BUDGET	ACTUAL
TOTAL:		

SAVINGS

DESCRIPTION	BUDGET
TOTAL:	

EXPENSES

DESCRIPTION	BUDGET	ACTUAL	DIFFERENCE
TOTAL:			

BUDGET *Planner*

MONTH:

STARTING BALANCE: _____

INCOME

DESCRIPTION	BUDGET	ACTUAL
TOTAL:		

SAVINGS

DESCRIPTION	BUDGET
TOTAL:	

EXPENSES

DESCRIPTION	BUDGET	ACTUAL	DIFFERENCE
TOTAL:			

BUDGET Planner

MONTH:

STARTING BALANCE: _____

INCOME

DESCRIPTION	BUDGET	ACTUAL
TOTAL:		

SAVINGS

DESCRIPTION	BUDGET
TOTAL:	

EXPENSES

DESCRIPTION	BUDGET	ACTUAL	DIFFERENCE
TOTAL:			

BUDGET *Planner*

MONTH:

STARTING BALANCE: _____

INCOME		
DESCRIPTION	BUDGET	ACTUAL
TOTAL:		

SAVINGS	
DESCRIPTION	BUDGET
TOTAL:	

EXPENSES			
DESCRIPTION	BUDGET	ACTUAL	DIFFERENCE
TOTAL:			

BUDGET *Planner*

MONTH:

STARTING BALANCE: _____

INCOME

DESCRIPTION	BUDGET	ACTUAL
TOTAL:		

SAVINGS

DESCRIPTION	BUDGET
TOTAL:	

EXPENSES

DESCRIPTION	BUDGET	ACTUAL	DIFFERENCE
TOTAL:			

BUDGET *Planner*

MONTH:

STARTING BALANCE: _____

INCOME

DESCRIPTION	BUDGET	ACTUAL
TOTAL:		

SAVINGS

DESCRIPTION	BUDGET
TOTAL:	

EXPENSES

DESCRIPTION	BUDGET	ACTUAL	DIFFERENCE
TOTAL:			

BUDGET *Planner*

MONTH:

STARTING BALANCE: _____

INCOME

DESCRIPTION	BUDGET	ACTUAL
TOTAL:		

SAVINGS

DESCRIPTION	BUDGET
TOTAL:	

EXPENSES

DESCRIPTION	BUDGET	ACTUAL	DIFFERENCE
TOTAL:			

BUDGET *Planner*

MONTH:

STARTING BALANCE: _____

INCOME

DESCRIPTION	BUDGET	ACTUAL
TOTAL:		

SAVINGS

DESCRIPTION	BUDGET
TOTAL:	

EXPENSES

DESCRIPTION	BUDGET	ACTUAL	DIFFERENCE
TOTAL:			

BUDGET *Planner*

MONTH:

STARTING BALANCE: _____

INCOME		
DESCRIPTION	BUDGET	ACTUAL
TOTAL:		

SAVINGS	
DESCRIPTION	BUDGET
TOTAL:	

EXPENSES			
DESCRIPTION	BUDGET	ACTUAL	DIFFERENCE
TOTAL:			

BUDGET *Planner*

MONTH:

STARTING BALANCE: _____

INCOME

DESCRIPTION	BUDGET	ACTUAL
TOTAL:		

SAVINGS

DESCRIPTION	BUDGET
TOTAL:	

EXPENSES

DESCRIPTION	BUDGET	ACTUAL	DIFFERENCE
TOTAL:			

BUDGET *Planner*

MONTH: _____

STARTING BALANCE: _____

INCOME

DESCRIPTION	BUDGET	ACTUAL
TOTAL:		

SAVINGS

DESCRIPTION	BUDGET
TOTAL:	

EXPENSES

DESCRIPTION	BUDGET	ACTUAL	DIFFERENCE
TOTAL:			

BUDGET *Planner*

MONTH:

STARTING BALANCE: _____

INCOME		
DESCRIPTION	BUDGET	ACTUAL
TOTAL:		

SAVINGS	
DESCRIPTION	BUDGET
TOTAL:	

EXPENSES			
DESCRIPTION	BUDGET	ACTUAL	DIFFERENCE
TOTAL:			

BUDGET *Planner*

MONTH:

STARTING BALANCE: _____

INCOME			SAVINGS	
DESCRIPTION	BUDGET	ACTUAL	DESCRIPTION	BUDGET
TOTAL:			TOTAL:	

EXPENSES			
DESCRIPTION	BUDGET	ACTUAL	DIFFERENCE
TOTAL:			

BUDGET *Planner*

MONTH:

STARTING BALANCE: _____

INCOME			SAVINGS	
DESCRIPTION	BUDGET	ACTUAL	DESCRIPTION	BUDGET
TOTAL:			**TOTAL:**	

EXPENSES			
DESCRIPTION	BUDGET	ACTUAL	DIFFERENCE
TOTAL:			

BUDGET *Planner*

MONTH:

STARTING BALANCE: _____

INCOME

DESCRIPTION	BUDGET	ACTUAL
TOTAL:		

SAVINGS

DESCRIPTION	BUDGET
TOTAL:	

EXPENSES

DESCRIPTION	BUDGET	ACTUAL	DIFFERENCE
TOTAL:			

BUDGET *Planner*

MONTH:

STARTING BALANCE: _____

INCOME

DESCRIPTION	BUDGET	ACTUAL
TOTAL:		

SAVINGS

DESCRIPTION	BUDGET
TOTAL:	

EXPENSES

DESCRIPTION	BUDGET	ACTUAL	DIFFERENCE
TOTAL:			

BUDGET *Planner*

MONTH:

STARTING BALANCE: _____

INCOME

DESCRIPTION	BUDGET	ACTUAL
TOTAL:		

SAVINGS

DESCRIPTION	BUDGET
TOTAL:	

EXPENSES

DESCRIPTION	BUDGET	ACTUAL	DIFFERENCE
TOTAL:			

BUDGET *Planner*

MONTH:

STARTING BALANCE: _____

INCOME

DESCRIPTION	BUDGET	ACTUAL

TOTAL:

SAVINGS

DESCRIPTION	BUDGET

TOTAL:

EXPENSES

DESCRIPTION	BUDGET	ACTUAL	DIFFERENCE

TOTAL:

BUDGET *Planner*

MONTH: _____

STARTING BALANCE: _____

INCOME

DESCRIPTION	BUDGET	ACTUAL
TOTAL:		

SAVINGS

DESCRIPTION	BUDGET
TOTAL:	

EXPENSES

DESCRIPTION	BUDGET	ACTUAL	DIFFERENCE
TOTAL:			

BUDGET *Planner*

MONTH:

STARTING BALANCE: _____

INCOME		
DESCRIPTION	BUDGET	ACTUAL
TOTAL:		

SAVINGS	
DESCRIPTION	BUDGET
TOTAL:	

EXPENSES			
DESCRIPTION	BUDGET	ACTUAL	DIFFERENCE
TOTAL:			

BUDGET *Planner*

MONTH:

STARTING BALANCE:

INCOME

DESCRIPTION	BUDGET	ACTUAL
TOTAL:		

SAVINGS

DESCRIPTION	BUDGET
TOTAL:	

EXPENSES

DESCRIPTION	BUDGET	ACTUAL	DIFFERENCE
TOTAL:			

BUDGET *Planner*

MONTH:

STARTING BALANCE: _____

INCOME			SAVINGS	
DESCRIPTION	BUDGET	ACTUAL	DESCRIPTION	BUDGET
TOTAL:			TOTAL:	

EXPENSES			
DESCRIPTION	BUDGET	ACTUAL	DIFFERENCE
TOTAL:			

BUDGET *Planner*

STARTING BALANCE: _____

INCOME

DESCRIPTION	BUDGET	ACTUAL
TOTAL:		

SAVINGS

DESCRIPTION	BUDGET
TOTAL:	

EXPENSES

DESCRIPTION	BUDGET	ACTUAL	DIFFERENCE
TOTAL:			

BUDGET *Planner*

MONTH:

STARTING BALANCE: _____

INCOME

DESCRIPTION	BUDGET	ACTUAL
TOTAL:		

SAVINGS

DESCRIPTION	BUDGET
TOTAL:	

EXPENSES

DESCRIPTION	BUDGET	ACTUAL	DIFFERENCE
TOTAL:			

BUDGET *Planner*

MONTH:

STARTING BALANCE: _____

INCOME

DESCRIPTION	BUDGET	ACTUAL
TOTAL:		

SAVINGS

DESCRIPTION	BUDGET
TOTAL:	

EXPENSES

DESCRIPTION	BUDGET	ACTUAL	DIFFERENCE
TOTAL:			

BUDGET *Planner*

MONTH:

STARTING BALANCE: _____

INCOME

DESCRIPTION	BUDGET	ACTUAL
TOTAL:		

SAVINGS

DESCRIPTION	BUDGET
TOTAL:	

EXPENSES

DESCRIPTION	BUDGET	ACTUAL	DIFFERENCE
TOTAL:			

BUDGET *Planner*

MONTH:

STARTING BALANCE: _____

INCOME

DESCRIPTION	BUDGET	ACTUAL
TOTAL:		

SAVINGS

DESCRIPTION	BUDGET
TOTAL:	

EXPENSES

DESCRIPTION	BUDGET	ACTUAL	DIFFERENCE
TOTAL:			

BUDGET *Planner*

MONTH:

STARTING BALANCE: _____

INCOME

DESCRIPTION	BUDGET	ACTUAL
TOTAL:		

SAVINGS

DESCRIPTION	BUDGET
TOTAL:	

EXPENSES

DESCRIPTION	BUDGET	ACTUAL	DIFFERENCE
TOTAL:			

BUDGET *Planner*

MONTH:

STARTING BALANCE: _____

INCOME

DESCRIPTION	BUDGET	ACTUAL
TOTAL:		

SAVINGS

DESCRIPTION	BUDGET
TOTAL:	

EXPENSES

DESCRIPTION	BUDGET	ACTUAL	DIFFERENCE
TOTAL:			

BUDGET *Planner*

MONTH:

STARTING BALANCE: _____

INCOME

DESCRIPTION	BUDGET	ACTUAL
TOTAL:		

SAVINGS

DESCRIPTION	BUDGET
TOTAL:	

EXPENSES

DESCRIPTION	BUDGET	ACTUAL	DIFFERENCE
TOTAL:			

BUDGET *Planner*

MONTH:

STARTING BALANCE:

INCOME

DESCRIPTION	BUDGET	ACTUAL
TOTAL:		

SAVINGS

DESCRIPTION	BUDGET
TOTAL:	

EXPENSES

DESCRIPTION	BUDGET	ACTUAL	DIFFERENCE
TOTAL:			

BUDGET *Planner*

MONTH:

STARTING BALANCE: _____

INCOME				SAVINGS	
DESCRIPTION	BUDGET	ACTUAL		DESCRIPTION	BUDGET
TOTAL:				TOTAL:	

EXPENSES			
DESCRIPTION	BUDGET	ACTUAL	DIFFERENCE
TOTAL:			

BUDGET *Planner*

MONTH:

STARTING BALANCE: _____

INCOME

DESCRIPTION	BUDGET	ACTUAL
TOTAL:		

SAVINGS

DESCRIPTION	BUDGET
TOTAL:	

EXPENSES

DESCRIPTION	BUDGET	ACTUAL	DIFFERENCE
TOTAL:			

BUDGET *Planner*

MONTH:

STARTING BALANCE: _____

INCOME

DESCRIPTION	BUDGET	ACTUAL
TOTAL:		

SAVINGS

DESCRIPTION	BUDGET
TOTAL:	

EXPENSES

DESCRIPTION	BUDGET	ACTUAL	DIFFERENCE
TOTAL:			

BUDGET *Planner*

MONTH:

STARTING BALANCE: _____

INCOME		
DESCRIPTION	BUDGET	ACTUAL
TOTAL:		

SAVINGS	
DESCRIPTION	BUDGET
TOTAL:	

EXPENSES			
DESCRIPTION	BUDGET	ACTUAL	DIFFERENCE
TOTAL:			

BUDGET *Planner*

MONTH:

STARTING BALANCE: _____

INCOME		
DESCRIPTION	BUDGET	ACTUAL
TOTAL:		

SAVINGS	
DESCRIPTION	BUDGET
TOTAL:	

EXPENSES			
DESCRIPTION	BUDGET	ACTUAL	DIFFERENCE
TOTAL:			

BUDGET *Planner*

MONTH:

STARTING BALANCE: _____

INCOME

DESCRIPTION	BUDGET	ACTUAL
TOTAL:		

SAVINGS

DESCRIPTION	BUDGET
TOTAL:	

EXPENSES

DESCRIPTION	BUDGET	ACTUAL	DIFFERENCE
TOTAL:			

BUDGET *Planner*

MONTH:

STARTING BALANCE: _____

INCOME				SAVINGS	
DESCRIPTION	BUDGET	ACTUAL		DESCRIPTION	BUDGET
TOTAL:				TOTAL:	

EXPENSES			
DESCRIPTION	BUDGET	ACTUAL	DIFFERENCE
TOTAL:			

BUDGET *Planner*

MONTH:

STARTING BALANCE: _____

INCOME

DESCRIPTION	BUDGET	ACTUAL
TOTAL:		

SAVINGS

DESCRIPTION	BUDGET
TOTAL:	

EXPENSES

DESCRIPTION	BUDGET	ACTUAL	DIFFERENCE
TOTAL:			

BUDGET *Planner*

MONTH:

STARTING BALANCE: _____

INCOME

DESCRIPTION	BUDGET	ACTUAL
TOTAL:		

SAVINGS

DESCRIPTION	BUDGET
TOTAL:	

EXPENSES

DESCRIPTION	BUDGET	ACTUAL	DIFFERENCE
TOTAL:			

BUDGET *Planner*

STARTING BALANCE: _____

INCOME				SAVINGS	
DESCRIPTION	BUDGET	ACTUAL		DESCRIPTION	BUDGET
TOTAL:				**TOTAL:**	

EXPENSES			
DESCRIPTION	BUDGET	ACTUAL	DIFFERENCE
TOTAL:			

BUDGET *Planner*

MONTH:

STARTING BALANCE: _____

INCOME		
DESCRIPTION	BUDGET	ACTUAL
TOTAL:		

SAVINGS	
DESCRIPTION	BUDGET
TOTAL:	

EXPENSES			
DESCRIPTION	BUDGET	ACTUAL	DIFFERENCE
TOTAL:			

BUDGET *Planner*

MONTH:

STARTING BALANCE: _____

INCOME

DESCRIPTION	BUDGET	ACTUAL
TOTAL:		

SAVINGS

DESCRIPTION	BUDGET
TOTAL:	

EXPENSES

DESCRIPTION	BUDGET	ACTUAL	DIFFERENCE
TOTAL:			

BUDGET *Planner*

MONTH:

STARTING BALANCE: _____

INCOME

DESCRIPTION	BUDGET	ACTUAL
TOTAL:		

SAVINGS

DESCRIPTION	BUDGET
TOTAL:	

EXPENSES

DESCRIPTION	BUDGET	ACTUAL	DIFFERENCE
TOTAL:			

BUDGET *Planner*

MONTH:

STARTING BALANCE: _____

INCOME			SAVINGS	
DESCRIPTION	BUDGET	ACTUAL	DESCRIPTION	BUDGET
TOTAL:			TOTAL:	

EXPENSES			
DESCRIPTION	BUDGET	ACTUAL	DIFFERENCE
TOTAL:			

BUDGET *Planner*

MONTH:

STARTING BALANCE: _____

INCOME		
DESCRIPTION	BUDGET	ACTUAL
TOTAL:		

SAVINGS	
DESCRIPTION	BUDGET
TOTAL:	

EXPENSES			
DESCRIPTION	BUDGET	ACTUAL	DIFFERENCE
TOTAL:			

BUDGET *Planner*

MONTH: _____

STARTING BALANCE: _____

INCOME

DESCRIPTION	BUDGET	ACTUAL
TOTAL:		

SAVINGS

DESCRIPTION	BUDGET
TOTAL:	

EXPENSES

DESCRIPTION	BUDGET	ACTUAL	DIFFERENCE
TOTAL:			

BUDGET *Planner*

MONTH:

STARTING BALANCE: _____

INCOME		
DESCRIPTION	BUDGET	ACTUAL
TOTAL:		

SAVINGS	
DESCRIPTION	BUDGET
TOTAL:	

EXPENSES			
DESCRIPTION	BUDGET	ACTUAL	DIFFERENCE
TOTAL:			

BUDGET *Planner*

MONTH:

STARTING BALANCE: _____

INCOME

DESCRIPTION	BUDGET	ACTUAL
TOTAL:		

SAVINGS

DESCRIPTION	BUDGET
TOTAL:	

EXPENSES

DESCRIPTION	BUDGET	ACTUAL	DIFFERENCE
TOTAL:			

BUDGET *Planner*

MONTH:

STARTING BALANCE:

INCOME

DESCRIPTION	BUDGET	ACTUAL
TOTAL:		

SAVINGS

DESCRIPTION	BUDGET
TOTAL:	

EXPENSES

DESCRIPTION	BUDGET	ACTUAL	DIFFERENCE
TOTAL:			

BUDGET *Planner*

MONTH: _____

STARTING BALANCE: _____

INCOME				SAVINGS	
DESCRIPTION	BUDGET	ACTUAL		DESCRIPTION	BUDGET
TOTAL:				**TOTAL:**	

EXPENSES			
DESCRIPTION	BUDGET	ACTUAL	DIFFERENCE
TOTAL:			

BUDGET *Planner*

MONTH:

STARTING BALANCE: _____

INCOME		
DESCRIPTION	BUDGET	ACTUAL
TOTAL:		

SAVINGS	
DESCRIPTION	BUDGET
TOTAL:	

EXPENSES			
DESCRIPTION	BUDGET	ACTUAL	DIFFERENCE
TOTAL:			

BUDGET *Planner*

MONTH:

STARTING BALANCE: _____

INCOME			SAVINGS	
DESCRIPTION	BUDGET	ACTUAL	DESCRIPTION	BUDGET
TOTAL:			TOTAL:	

EXPENSES			
DESCRIPTION	BUDGET	ACTUAL	DIFFERENCE
TOTAL:			

BUDGET *Planner*

MONTH:

STARTING BALANCE: _____

INCOME

DESCRIPTION	BUDGET	ACTUAL
TOTAL:		

SAVINGS

DESCRIPTION	BUDGET
TOTAL:	

EXPENSES

DESCRIPTION	BUDGET	ACTUAL	DIFFERENCE
TOTAL:			

BUDGET *Planner*

MONTH:

STARTING BALANCE: _____

INCOME

DESCRIPTION	BUDGET	ACTUAL
TOTAL:		

SAVINGS

DESCRIPTION	BUDGET
TOTAL:	

EXPENSES

DESCRIPTION	BUDGET	ACTUAL	DIFFERENCE
TOTAL:			

BUDGET *Planner*

MONTH:

STARTING BALANCE: _____

INCOME

DESCRIPTION	BUDGET	ACTUAL
TOTAL:		

SAVINGS

DESCRIPTION	BUDGET
TOTAL:	

EXPENSES

DESCRIPTION	BUDGET	ACTUAL	DIFFERENCE
TOTAL:			

BUDGET *Planner*

MONTH:

STARTING BALANCE: _____

INCOME		
DESCRIPTION	BUDGET	ACTUAL
TOTAL:		

SAVINGS	
DESCRIPTION	BUDGET
TOTAL:	

EXPENSES			
DESCRIPTION	BUDGET	ACTUAL	DIFFERENCE
TOTAL:			

BUDGET *Planner*

MONTH:

STARTING BALANCE: _____

INCOME

DESCRIPTION	BUDGET	ACTUAL
TOTAL:		

SAVINGS

DESCRIPTION	BUDGET
TOTAL:	

EXPENSES

DESCRIPTION	BUDGET	ACTUAL	DIFFERENCE
TOTAL:			

BUDGET *Planner*

MONTH:

STARTING BALANCE: _____

INCOME

DESCRIPTION	BUDGET	ACTUAL
TOTAL:		

SAVINGS

DESCRIPTION	BUDGET
TOTAL:	

EXPENSES

DESCRIPTION	BUDGET	ACTUAL	DIFFERENCE
TOTAL:			

BUDGET Planner

MONTH:

STARTING BALANCE: _____

INCOME

DESCRIPTION	BUDGET	ACTUAL
TOTAL:		

SAVINGS

DESCRIPTION	BUDGET
TOTAL:	

EXPENSES

DESCRIPTION	BUDGET	ACTUAL	DIFFERENCE
TOTAL:			

BUDGET *Planner*

MONTH:

STARTING BALANCE: _____

INCOME

DESCRIPTION	BUDGET	ACTUAL
TOTAL:		

SAVINGS

DESCRIPTION	BUDGET
TOTAL:	

EXPENSES

DESCRIPTION	BUDGET	ACTUAL	DIFFERENCE
TOTAL:			

BUDGET *Planner*

MONTH:

STARTING BALANCE: _____

INCOME

DESCRIPTION	BUDGET	ACTUAL
TOTAL:		

SAVINGS

DESCRIPTION	BUDGET
TOTAL:	

EXPENSES

DESCRIPTION	BUDGET	ACTUAL	DIFFERENCE
TOTAL:			

BUDGET *Planner*

MONTH: _____

STARTING BALANCE: _____

INCOME				SAVINGS	
DESCRIPTION	BUDGET	ACTUAL		DESCRIPTION	BUDGET
TOTAL:				TOTAL:	

EXPENSES			
DESCRIPTION	BUDGET	ACTUAL	DIFFERENCE
TOTAL:			

BUDGET *Planner*

MONTH:

STARTING BALANCE: _____

INCOME

DESCRIPTION	BUDGET	ACTUAL
TOTAL:		

SAVINGS

DESCRIPTION	BUDGET
TOTAL:	

EXPENSES

DESCRIPTION	BUDGET	ACTUAL	DIFFERENCE
TOTAL:			

BUDGET *Planner*

MONTH:

STARTING BALANCE: _____

INCOME

DESCRIPTION	BUDGET	ACTUAL
TOTAL:		

SAVINGS

DESCRIPTION	BUDGET
TOTAL:	

EXPENSES

DESCRIPTION	BUDGET	ACTUAL	DIFFERENCE
TOTAL:			

BUDGET Planner

MONTH:

STARTING BALANCE:

INCOME

DESCRIPTION	BUDGET	ACTUAL
TOTAL:		

SAVINGS

DESCRIPTION	BUDGET
TOTAL:	

EXPENSES

DESCRIPTION	BUDGET	ACTUAL	DIFFERENCE
TOTAL:			

BUDGET *Planner*

MONTH:

STARTING BALANCE: _____

INCOME

DESCRIPTION	BUDGET	ACTUAL
TOTAL:		

SAVINGS

DESCRIPTION	BUDGET
TOTAL:	

EXPENSES

DESCRIPTION	BUDGET	ACTUAL	DIFFERENCE
TOTAL:			

BUDGET *Planner*

MONTH:

STARTING BALANCE: _____

INCOME

DESCRIPTION	BUDGET	ACTUAL
TOTAL:		

SAVINGS

DESCRIPTION	BUDGET
TOTAL:	

EXPENSES

DESCRIPTION	BUDGET	ACTUAL	DIFFERENCE
TOTAL:			

BUDGET *Planner*

MONTH: _____

STARTING BALANCE: _____

INCOME

DESCRIPTION	BUDGET	ACTUAL
TOTAL:		

SAVINGS

DESCRIPTION	BUDGET
TOTAL:	

EXPENSES

DESCRIPTION	BUDGET	ACTUAL	DIFFERENCE
TOTAL:			

BUDGET *Planner*

MONTH:

STARTING BALANCE: _____

INCOME			SAVINGS	
DESCRIPTION	BUDGET	ACTUAL	DESCRIPTION	BUDGET
TOTAL:			TOTAL:	

EXPENSES			
DESCRIPTION	BUDGET	ACTUAL	DIFFERENCE
TOTAL:			

BUDGET *Planner*

MONTH:

STARTING BALANCE: _____

INCOME

DESCRIPTION	BUDGET	ACTUAL
TOTAL:		

SAVINGS

DESCRIPTION	BUDGET
TOTAL:	

EXPENSES

DESCRIPTION	BUDGET	ACTUAL	DIFFERENCE
TOTAL:			

BUDGET *Planner*

STARTING BALANCE: _____

INCOME

DESCRIPTION	BUDGET	ACTUAL
TOTAL:		

SAVINGS

DESCRIPTION	BUDGET
TOTAL:	

EXPENSES

DESCRIPTION	BUDGET	ACTUAL	DIFFERENCE
TOTAL:			

BUDGET *Planner*

MONTH:

STARTING BALANCE: _____

INCOME

DESCRIPTION	BUDGET	ACTUAL
TOTAL:		

SAVINGS

DESCRIPTION	BUDGET
TOTAL:	

EXPENSES

DESCRIPTION	BUDGET	ACTUAL	DIFFERENCE
TOTAL:			

BUDGET *Planner*

MONTH:

STARTING BALANCE: _____

INCOME			SAVINGS	
DESCRIPTION	BUDGET	ACTUAL	DESCRIPTION	BUDGET
TOTAL:			TOTAL:	

EXPENSES			
DESCRIPTION	BUDGET	ACTUAL	DIFFERENCE
TOTAL:			

BUDGET *Planner*

MONTH: _____

STARTING BALANCE: _____

INCOME

DESCRIPTION	BUDGET	ACTUAL
TOTAL:		

SAVINGS

DESCRIPTION	BUDGET
TOTAL:	

EXPENSES

DESCRIPTION	BUDGET	ACTUAL	DIFFERENCE
TOTAL:			

BUDGET *Planner*

MONTH:

STARTING BALANCE: _____

INCOME

DESCRIPTION	BUDGET	ACTUAL
TOTAL:		

SAVINGS

DESCRIPTION	BUDGET
TOTAL:	

EXPENSES

DESCRIPTION	BUDGET	ACTUAL	DIFFERENCE
TOTAL:			

BUDGET *Planner*

MONTH:

STARTING BALANCE: _____

INCOME

DESCRIPTION	BUDGET	ACTUAL
TOTAL:		

SAVINGS

DESCRIPTION	BUDGET
TOTAL:	

EXPENSES

DESCRIPTION	BUDGET	ACTUAL	DIFFERENCE
TOTAL:			

BUDGET *Planner*

MONTH:

STARTING BALANCE: _____

INCOME		
DESCRIPTION	BUDGET	ACTUAL
TOTAL:		

SAVINGS	
DESCRIPTION	BUDGET
TOTAL:	

EXPENSES			
DESCRIPTION	BUDGET	ACTUAL	DIFFERENCE
TOTAL:			

BUDGET *Planner*

MONTH:

STARTING BALANCE: _____

INCOME

DESCRIPTION	BUDGET	ACTUAL
TOTAL:		

SAVINGS

DESCRIPTION	BUDGET
TOTAL:	

EXPENSES

DESCRIPTION	BUDGET	ACTUAL	DIFFERENCE
TOTAL:			

BUDGET *Planner*

MONTH:

STARTING BALANCE: _____

INCOME

DESCRIPTION	BUDGET	ACTUAL
TOTAL:		

SAVINGS

DESCRIPTION	BUDGET
TOTAL:	

EXPENSES

DESCRIPTION	BUDGET	ACTUAL	DIFFERENCE
TOTAL:			

BUDGET *Planner*

MONTH:

STARTING BALANCE: _____

INCOME			SAVINGS	
DESCRIPTION	BUDGET	ACTUAL	DESCRIPTION	BUDGET
TOTAL:			TOTAL:	

EXPENSES			
DESCRIPTION	BUDGET	ACTUAL	DIFFERENCE
TOTAL:			

BUDGET *Planner*

MONTH: _____

STARTING BALANCE: _____

INCOME

DESCRIPTION	BUDGET	ACTUAL
TOTAL:		

SAVINGS

DESCRIPTION	BUDGET
TOTAL:	

EXPENSES

DESCRIPTION	BUDGET	ACTUAL	DIFFERENCE
TOTAL:			

BUDGET *Planner*

MONTH:

STARTING BALANCE: _____

INCOME				SAVINGS	
DESCRIPTION	BUDGET	ACTUAL		DESCRIPTION	BUDGET
TOTAL:				TOTAL:	

EXPENSES			
DESCRIPTION	BUDGET	ACTUAL	DIFFERENCE
TOTAL:			

BUDGET *Planner*

MONTH:

STARTING BALANCE: _____

INCOME			SAVINGS	
DESCRIPTION	BUDGET	ACTUAL	DESCRIPTION	BUDGET
TOTAL:			TOTAL:	

EXPENSES			
DESCRIPTION	BUDGET	ACTUAL	DIFFERENCE
TOTAL: